Catholic Marriage

An Intimate Community of Life and Love

Patricia Murphy

© 2011 Novalis Publishing Inc.

Nihil Obstat: Suzanne Rozell Scorsone, Ph.D.
Archdiocese of Toronto
3 February 2011

Imprimatur: +Thomas Collins
Archbishop of Toronto
3 February 2011

Cover design and layout: Audrey Wells

Published by Novalis

Publishing Office
10 Lower Spadina Avenue, Suite 400
Toronto, Ontario, Canada
M5V 2Z2

Head Office
4475 Frontenac Street
Montréal, Québec, Canada
H2H 2S2

www.novalis.ca

Library and Archives Canada Cataloguing in Publication

Murphy, Patricia
  Catholic marriage : an intimate community of life and love / Patricia Murphy.

Issued also in electronic format. ISBN 978-2-89646-235-3

  1. Marriage--Religious aspects--Catholic Church. I. Title.

BX2250.M87 2011   234'.165   C2010-908020-3

Printed in Canada.

All rights reserved. No part of this publication may be reproduced, stored in a retrieval system, or transmitted in any form, or by any means, electronic, mechanical, photocopying, recording, or otherwise, without the written permission of the publisher.

The Scripture quotations contained herein are from the Revised Standard Version of the Bible, copyrighted 1952 by the Division of Christian Education of the National Council of the Churches of Christ in the United States of America, and are used by permission.

We acknowledge the financial support of the Government of Canada through the Canada Book Fund for business development activities.

Contents

Introduction: Beyond "Bridezilla" 4

1. A Whirlwind Tour: The Story of Our Salvation 7
2. Life in Christ: Everyone Is Invited to the Banquet 17
3. Marriage "in the Lord": What's Different About Christian Marriage? 26
4. Sacramental Marriage: How Do We Live It? 39
5. Is Any of This Possible? Can We Really Love As Christ Loves? 54

Conclusion 61

Notes 63

Introduction

Beyond "Bridezilla"

Sometimes it seems that the world has gone wedding crazy. Turn on the TV any evening and there is a good chance you will find a reality show dedicated to some aspect of planning the perfect wedding. One night the focus might be on the stressed-out and cranky bride – also known as "Bridezilla." Another night might look at the ever-growing wedding budget, or the opinionated future mother-in-law. There are even shows about saying "yes" to the perfect dress – and to cake masterpieces that would put the architects of the Empire State Building to shame. An entire industry is now devoted to making the big day more special than any bride or groom ever imagined – for a price. And as the TV viewer ratings show, many of us are fascinated by it all.

With so many options and expectations for weddings, is it any wonder that today's engaged couples feel overwhelmed? (Maybe that's why the destination wedding, with lots of beach and few formalities, is becoming so popular.) In the midst of all the extreme planning, should we be surprised if the bride- and groom-to-be can find little or no time to focus on things that will matter long after the guests have had their last glass of New Zealand Pinot Noir? As everyone knows, it is easy to get swept up in all the details of the wedding day.

Let's face it. Everyone but the world's biggest grinch agrees that weddings are a very big deal. They deserve to be planned with care and they are surely among the most joyful and important events celebrated in virtually all cultures, throughout the ages. We even have it on the Bible's good authority that Jesus himself understood the deep significance of a wedding. After all, it was at the wedding feast at Cana that he performed his first sign, turning jars of water into wine when the host's supply ran out.

But as the saying goes, a wedding is one day; a marriage is forever. That's why couples, even as they plan their wedding day, must spend time preparing for their marriage.

The Catholic Church takes marriage very seriously. In fact, the Church teaches that the valid marriage of two Christians is a *sacrament*. During the wedding ceremony, a man and woman vow to love each other as Christ loves us. Their marriage becomes a symbol of – and participation in – Christ's own divine love. For this reason, the Church and all its members share in the joy of each wedding feast, as Christ did at Cana.

Still, many Catholics find it hard to explain exactly what it means to say that marriage is a sacrament. They may not know how to answer when friends, neighbours or colleagues ask them questions such as: Why must marriage be for life? Why can't Catholics get divorced and remarry? Is a Catholic marriage really so different from a non-Catholic marriage? Why do people who get married in the Catholic Church have to agree to be open to the gift of children? Is that really any of the Church's business?

It is hard to speak intelligently about these issues if we do not have a strong grasp of the basic teachings of our faith.

This book was inspired by the fact that many people would like to learn more about the basics of their faith: creation, sin, the person of Christ and his redemptive work, the origin and mission of the Church, the sacraments, what it means to be human, and more. The sacramental nature of marriage makes more sense once the basics are in place.

We will explore this subject by presenting the Church's teaching on marriage organically or holistically – as part of what you might call a mini Theology 101 course for busy people like you. The aim is simply to consider marriage "in the Lord" in positive terms, rather than responding directly to all of the challenges to marriage today.

The *Catechism of the Catholic Church* (CCC) will be our guide. The *Catechism* is an indispensable theological GPS for anyone who has embarked on the lifelong journey (and adventure) that is the Catholic faith. Much of what is introduced here is treated in a more detailed manner in the *Catechism* itself. It is my hope that this book will encourage you to have a deeper encounter with that tremendous resource and with others I will mention.

While I draw heavily on the *Catechism*, the approach I take here also reflects the fact that faith and reason go hand in hand. Catholics say that grace perfects nature and that faith does not annihilate or destroy reason, but enlightens reason. This means, as we will see, that in matters relating to human life and love, the light of faith often confirms basic truths that human reason and experience have identified.

Whether you are preparing for marriage or simply want to learn more about what it means to be Catholic, I hope this book will help you deepen your understanding of key elements of your faith, especially the sacrament of marriage.

I

A Whirlwind Tour: The Story of Our Salvation

If you have asked to be married in the Catholic Church, to be married "in the Lord," there is no better time than the present to ask yourselves, "Why the Catholic Church?" Of course, to be able to give an honest answer, you need to have some understanding of what the Catholic Church is. Many people have said that to speak about the Church is to speak about the person of Christ. In speaking of Christ, we come face to face with the "good news" of our salvation – news that turns out to be infinitely better than anything we could ever have imagined for ourselves!

This chapter gives a brief overview of some key truths of our salvation history. This overview will set the stage for the rest of the book.

The Trinity: One God in three persons

Whenever we as Christians bless ourselves, we do so "in the name of the Father, and of the Son, and of the Holy Spirit." We do this because our faith teaches that the mystery of the Trinity is the "central mystery of Christian faith and life" and the source of all other mysteries of the faith. (CCC #234) To believe in a God who is a trinity is not a matter of believing in three separate gods (that would be polytheism), but in *one God in three persons*. Each of the divine persons is truly God, whole and entire. And yet these divine persons (Father, Son and Holy Spirit) really are distinct from each other. They are distinct in their relations of origin: it is the Father who generates, the Son who is begotten, and the Holy Spirit who proceeds. (CCC #253–254)

Created in God's image

What does the Trinity have to do with marriage? The fact that God is a "community" of equal yet distinct persons has great significance for us people who are created in God's image.

Sacred scripture, what we call the Bible, presents the work of creation in a symbolic way. God does six days of divine work, and rests on the seventh day. (CCC #337) From the two creation stories (in the first two chapters of the Book of Genesis, Genesis 1 and Genesis 2) we learn that everything owes its existence to God the creator – and that when he looked upon all that he had made, God said it was "good" (or even "very good"). We also learn from these stories that humanity is unique among visible creatures: "man is the only creature on earth that God has willed for its own sake." (CCC #356, citing *Gaudium et Spes* #24)

The two creation accounts tell basic truths about humans. Genesis 1 says, "So God created humankind in his image, in the image of God he created them; male and female he created them." (verse 27) Then God blessed them and instructed them to be "fruitful" and to multiply. (verse 28)

Genesis 2 builds on these truths by describing the experience of the first man in more personal terms. God put him in the garden of Eden, which he was to cultivate. Then God said, "You may freely eat of every tree in the garden; but of the tree of the knowledge of good and evil you shall not eat, for in the day that you eat of it you shall die." (verses 16-17) Significantly, it was God who then declared, "It is not good that the man should be alone; I will give him a helper as his partner." Before doing so, however, God formed various birds and animals and brought them to the man so that the man could name them. Yet, as we are told, "there was not found a helper as his partner." So God cast a deep sleep over the man, took one of his ribs and formed a woman from the rib. When God brought the woman to the man, the man exclaimed, "This at last is bone of my bones and flesh of my flesh." The chapter ends by saying, "Therefore a man leaves his father and mother and clings to his wife, and they become one flesh. And the man and his wife were both naked, and were not ashamed." (verses 18-25)

What do we learn about ourselves from these truths? That we are made in God's own image is a stunning truth that we may sometimes take for granted. As God's image, the *imago dei*, we have spiritual capacities or "faculties" that make us capable of knowing and loving. The *Catechism* puts it this way:

> Being in the image of God the human individual possesses the dignity of a *person*, who is not just something, but someone. He is capable of self-knowledge, of self-possession, and of freely giving himself and entering into communion with other persons. And he is called by grace to a covenant with his Creator, to offer him a response of faith and love that no other creature can give in his stead. (#357)

In the past, theologians often stressed that we are most like God in the way we can think and choose. Although our intellect and will do separate us from rocks, plants and shrimp, the above passage reflects a deeper understanding of a fundamental human truth. Just as God is a community of persons, so we, made in God's image, are made to be in community with others – and, ultimately, with God.

These days, we hear a lot of talk about human dignity and the fact that we should never be "used" by others. The above passage reminds us that it is our vocation to participate in God's own life and love, which are the ultimate foundation of human dignity. No matter what a person's abilities, accomplishments or limits are, the fact that he or she exists means that he or she is a person in relationship with others and with God. This can only be a good thing.

The creation stories in the Bible also show that humans are both physical and spiritual beings. In traditional theological terms, the person is described as a "composite" of body and soul. As the *Catechism* puts it, "The biblical account expresses this reality in symbolic language when it affirms that 'then the Lord God formed man of dust from the ground, and breathed into his nostrils the breath of life; and man became a living being.'" (CCC #362, citing Genesis 2:7) The term "soul" can refer both to human life itself and to the person as a whole. "Soul" can also refer to the "spiritual principle" of a person, the part that is of the greatest value, by which the person most clearly images God. (CCC #363) As we know from the Bible, Adam and Eve had human, physical bodies. The Christian tradition has consistently declared that the body shares in the dignity of the human person. For example, both the Apostles' Creed and the Nicene Creed, which are official professions of Christian faith, state a belief in the resurrection of the human body. This is a truth that is often overlooked today. (Whether we like it or not, our body is coming with us after we die; the good news is that it will be a "glorified" body!)

Man and woman:
Created equal and complementary

Finally, our faith teaches that man and woman were created with equal dignity and as "partners." As we see in the creation stories, neither the man nor the woman is made "more" in the image of God. In fact, Genesis 2 makes it clear that man and woman were created together and *for* each other. The first man was "lonely," with no "suitable partner" until Eve came on the scene. When she appeared, he seemed to know right away that she was like him, and yet, as a woman, she was also different from him. And he was delighted! The *Catechism* sums up this point well:

> Man and woman were made "for each other" – not that God left them half-made and incomplete: he created them to be a communion of persons, in which each can be a "helpmate" to the other, for they are equal as persons ... and complementary as masculine and feminine. (CCC #372)

Gender is therefore no accident, and is not a superficial thing. Rather, our being created as female and male draws attention to the truth that we are created for the "other," for relationship. Because they complement each other physically and in other ways, a man and woman together are uniquely capable of forming "one flesh" (in sexual intercourse). In this way, they are together uniquely capable of transmitting human life, of being fruitful. You don't need to be a

Christian (or have any religious faith) to appreciate these basic truths about human nature.

Evil: How can we explain it?

But there is much more to the story. As wonderful as life is, we do not have to look far to see the suffering and injustice in our world. How did this happen? Why is there evil in the world?

Some people insist that all the world's problems and human failings are caused by ignorance or injustice in society. As the *Catechism* notes, many are tempted to explain evil only as the result of a "developmental flaw, a psychological weakness, a mistake, or the necessary consequences of an inadequate social structure." (CCC #387)

But Christians have always viewed the matter differently. We have seen that everything God created was "good." This includes the first man. God created him and established him in friendship, in what has also been called a state of "original holiness" and justice. As a spiritual creature made in God's image, the man was created with freedom – freedom to follow God's command or not. The *Catechism* explains it this way:

> The prohibition against eating "of the tree of the knowledge of good and evil" spells this out: "for in that day that you eat of it, you shall die." (Gen. 2:17) The "tree of the knowledge of good and evil" (Gen. 2:17) symbolically evokes the insurmountable limits that man, being a creature, must freely recognize and respect with trust. Man is dependent on his Creator and subject to the laws of creation and to the moral norms that govern the use of freedom. (CCC #396)

Sin: It's all about relationship

As we know, our first parents, Adam and Eve, did not follow God's command. They sinned: "Man, tempted by the devil, let his trust in his Creator die in his heart and, abusing his freedom, *disobeyed* God's command. This is what man's first sin consisted of. (Gen. 3:1-11) All subsequent sin would be disobedience toward God and lack of trust in his goodness." (CCC #397)

A Whirlwind Tour

This is what we call "original sin." The first sin was not a sexual sin, nor was it about eating apples from the wrong tree. (As we will see, this important truth can help us understand the goodness of sexuality within marriage.) Rather, the Genesis account uses symbolic language to explain that our first parents refused to accept their status as creatures, even though they were creatures who had been created for a most sublime destiny. Seduced by the devil's promises, they wanted to "be like God," but "without God." (CCC #398) That is why original sin is so often identified with a kind of pride.

Once the man and woman made it clear that they preferred their own agenda to God's, things quickly took a turn for the worse. The first break in their relationship with God caused them to lose the grace of "original holiness." They now feared God. This rupture echoed throughout creation in a variety of ways. Man and woman lost the inner personal harmony that had existed between their reason and their passions or emotions; "disordered desire" had entered the picture. The relations between the man and woman (who had been created *for* each other) were strained. They were now often coloured by lust, by the tendency to use or objectify the other, and by the desire to dominate the other. (Translation: the gender wars started.) Being stewards of the earth now meant struggle and toil. Childbirth now involved labour pains. Humanity's relationship with creation itself was harmed: we know all too well the toll that greed has taken on the planet. All of creation (including human life) became subject to "bondage and decay." (Genesis 3:19) Suffering and death became a "fact of life." (CCC #400, #1607)

Scripture and the Church's Tradition affirm that sin is present and pervasive in the world. These have taught that human misery – our inclination towards evil and death – can be explained only in light of Adam's first sin. This sin has since been transmitted to and has afflicted every member of the human family. (CCC #403)

We may ask: How is it that we, in the 21st century, are part of something that happened so long ago? We weren't even there! The short answer is that since we are all members of one human family, we are all somehow – but mysteriously – implicated in Adam's sin, just as we are all implicated in Christ's justice. We are born with a human

Catholic Marriage

nature that is not what it should be. Because it has been deprived of original holiness and justice, our nature is sometimes described as "fallen." (CCC #404)

It's worth pointing out that Adam and Eve committed a personal sin (one for which they alone were responsible). Although original sin affects each of us as individuals, it is not a personal sin or fault in us, Adam's descendants. For us, it is more accurate to describe original sin as a "state contracted" and not a personal act that we have done. So it is not technically "sin" according to the usual meaning of the word. (CCC #404) (This may help us answer those who wonder how we can speak of original sin when it comes to newborn babies, who couldn't possibly have done anything wrong – though they might sometimes keep their parents up all night!)

Still, we all feel the effects of humanity's wounded state. As the *Catechism* explains, human nature "is wounded in the natural powers proper to it; subject to ignorance, suffering and the dominion of death; and inclined to sin – an inclination to evil that is called 'concupiscence.'" (CCC #405) As we will see in the next chapter, the grace of baptism erases original sin, which restores our relationship with God. But it does not erase the consequences of a weakened nature that is inclined to evil. (CCC #405)

Grace: Drawing closer to God

A Catholic view of things involves a delicate balance of optimism and realism about human nature. Nature is wounded, but not destroyed. Even more important, it is both healed and elevated by grace. We are all works in progress. (We'll return to this point in Chapter 4.)

God always finds something he can work with in us. The central theme of our salvation history is that God tries over and over again to bring us closer to him. Over the millennia, God has communicated himself to us through the various stages of supernatural Revelation. Those stages culminated in the person and mission of Christ. (CCC #53) The main message of Revelation is that "God loves his people." (*Familiaris Consortio*, #12)

So God did not abandon man after the first sin. Instead, God reached out to humanity in many ways: he made a covenant with Noah after the Flood; he made Abraham the "father of a multitude of nations"; after the time of the patriarchs, he formed Israel as his people, freeing them from slavery in Egypt; and he made the covenant of Mount Sinai, giving the Israelites his law (the "terms" of this covenant) through Moses. (CCC #56–63)

The prophets were keenly aware of God's steadfast love. God used his prophets to give people the hope of salvation and redemption from all their sins. The people came to expect that God would one day create a new and everlasting covenant with them; as Jeremiah foretold, God would write this new covenant "on their hearts." (Jeremiah 31:33)

Redemption in Christ

You may be glad to hear that it is finally time to consider the "good news" of Christ and the new covenant he has established. What sets Christian faith apart is the belief in the unique and unrepeatable event of the Incarnation. The Incarnation recognizes that the Son of God took on a human nature in order to bring about our salvation. (CCC #461) As the Nicene Creed states,

> We believe in one Lord, Jesus Christ, the only Son of God, eternally begotten of the Father ... one in Being with the Father ... For us men and our salvation he came down from heaven: by the power of the Holy Spirit he was born of the Virgin Mary, and became man. For our sake he was crucified under Pontius Pilate; he suffered, died and was buried. On the third day he rose again in fulfillment of the Scriptures ....

Christians believe that Christ became truly man while remaining truly God. This does not mean that Jesus Christ is part God and part man. It also does not mean he is some kind of "confused mixture" of the divine and the human. Rather, Christ's humanity has no other subject than the divine person of the only-begotten Son. Christ is therefore one divine person acknowledged in two natures (one human and one divine). (CCC #464–469) For this reason, he is the only mediator between God and us.

Why did God's Son become one of us? He did so for our salvation, to reconcile us with God the Father though his suffering and death. He also became fully human so that we might know God's love; to be our model of holiness; and to make us "partakers of the divine nature." (CCC #456-460) Thomas Aquinas, a great medieval theologian, explains this point well: "The only-begotten Son of God, wanting to make us sharers in his divinity, assumed our nature, so that he, made man, might make men Gods." (CCC #460, citing Aquinas)

Christ's gift of self:
The triumph of life over death

But how was such a thing possible? Our redemption is not something we could earn or deserve, but is pure gift or grace. (CCC #604) Although Christ was without sin, he *freely* and obediently took upon himself all the sin and suffering of the world; he then offered it all to his Father, through his own unfathomable suffering and death on the cross. As St. Paul said, "For just as by the one man's disobedience the many were made sinners, so by the one man's obedience the many will be made righteous." (Romans 5:19)

"It is 'love to the end' (John 13:1) that confers on Christ's sacrifice its value as redemption and reparation, as atonement and satisfaction." (CCC #616) Pope John Paul II says this of Christ's "total gift of self," his suffering and death for us:

> In His suffering, sins are cancelled out precisely because He alone as the only-begotten Son could take them upon Himself, accept them *with that love for the Father which overcomes the evil of every sin;* in a certain sense he annihilates this evil in the spiritual space of the relationship between God and humanity, and fills this space with good. (*Salvifici Doloris*, #17)

By joining his suffering to his unconditional love, Christ also changed the meaning of human suffering itself. Now, when we offer our suffering in love as a participation in Christ's own salvific suffering, it too can be in the service of true good.[1]

The passion and death of Jesus on Good Friday were anything but the last word. These are followed by Easter Sunday, by Christ's resurrection! This triumph of life over death is a confirmation of all

Christ's works and teachings and his divinity. It is the fulfillment of God's promises. It is the source of our own future resurrection. (CCC #651–655) As the *Catechism* says, "by his death, Christ liberates us from sin; by his Resurrection, he opens for us the way to a new life. This new life is above all *justification* that reinstates us in God's grace ... It brings about *filial adoption*." (CCC #654)

The Christian message: It can change the world

It is often said that the Christian message is a radical one. This may be an understatement! Our faith teaches that we are saved from all our individual and group messes not by power, not by violence, and not by education and technology (though these are important and must be put to good use). We are not even saved by a good and reasonable code of ethics or the example of very enlightened people. Sin is real. The experience of rupture in relationship with God and others is all too real. We simply can't fix the world and ourselves on our own. But there is good reason to hope. Christians believe that reconciliation (between us and God and among humans) is possible because of a real person, Christ, who made the ultimate gift of self for us.

In Chapter 2, we will explore how each of us has new life in Christ, and what that means for couples like you who are preparing for marriage.

2

Life in Christ: Everyone Is Invited to the Banquet

How do we enter new life in Christ? What does it look like? To answer these questions, we need to look at three things: the origin and mission of the Church, the sacrament of baptism, and the real-life implications of "life in Christ": the vocation each baptized person has to love as Christ loves, in his or her own unique way.

The Church: Given to us by Christ

The *Catechism* provides a very rich and extensive treatment of the Church (Article 9, #748–975). Here I will touch on just a few key points.

The mystery of the Church cannot be understood apart from the mission of Christ and the Holy Spirit. While he was on earth, Christ inaugurated his Church by preaching the Good News, the coming of the Reign of God. (CCC #763) He also gave his community of disciples a structure that will remain in place until the kingdom of God is fully achieved. This structure included, among other things, the choice of the twelve apostles, with Peter as their head. The twelve – and all the other disciples – share in Christ's mission and in his suffering. (CCC #765) Christ promised his disciples that after he was gone, the Father would send the Holy Spirit to help and guide them. (Their mission is interconnected: whenever the Father sends his Son, he always sends his Spirit.) In the Gospel of John, Christ says to his disciples, "the Advocate, the Holy Spirit, whom the Father will send in my name, will teach you everything, and remind you of all I have said to you." (John 14:26)

On the night before his passion, Christ transformed his final meal with his apostles (the Last Supper) into the memorial of his sacrifice for the salvation of people. And so at every Eucharist, we recall Christ's words: "This is my body, which is given for you." (Luke 22:19; Matthew 26:28) The next day, through his Paschal sacrifice (the sacrifice of the "Lamb of God, who takes away the sin of the world" [John 1:29; 1 Corinthians 5:7]), Christ made his definitive gift of self for his disciples and for each of us. (CCC #613)

The *Catechism* speaks of how the Church came to be, after Christ's death:

> The Church is born primarily of Christ's total self-giving for our salvation, anticipated in the institution of the Eucharist and fulfilled on the Cross ... As Eve was formed from the sleeping Adam's side, so the Church was born from the pierced heart of Christ hanging dead on the Cross. (CCC #766)

When Christ's work on earth was done, his promise to his community of disciples was fulfilled. From the Acts of the Apostles, which follows the Gospel of John in the Bible, we learn that on the day of Pentecost (at the end of seven weeks following Easter), the disciples had gathered together and the Holy Spirit was sent to them: "Divided tongues, as of fire, appeared among them, and a tongue rested on each of them. All of them were filled with the Holy Spirit and began to speak in other languages, as the Spirit gave them ability." (Acts 2:3-4) As the *Catechism* puts it, with the gift of the Holy Spirit, the Church was "openly displayed" to the world, and the spreading of the good news of God's love to all nations was begun. Now, in this "age of the Church," Christ lives and acts in and through his Church. As he promised, he has not left his disciples orphans. (CCC #767)

So that the Church could fulfill her mission to tell people of God's love for all, the Holy Spirit continually makes the Church holy and gives it various gifts. The Spirit also guides the Church's actions using these gifts. (CCC #768)

All of salvation history can be described as a "great mystery." In the Church, Christ fulfills and reveals his own mystery, which is to fulfill

God's plan "to unite all things in him." (CCC #772, citing Ephesians 1:10) The *Catechism* explains: "The one mediator, Christ, established and ever sustains here on earth his holy Church, the community of faith, hope and charity, as a visible organization though which he communicates truth and grace to all men." (CCC #771, citing *Lumen Gentium* #8) So profound is the Church's union with Christ, she also is a "mystery" in her own right. (CCC #772) Understood as a mystery, the Church is also "like a sacrament" – a sign and instrument by which Christ is "at once manifesting and actualizing the mystery of God's love for men." (CCC #775–776, citing *Lumen Gentium* #9:2, #48:2; *Gaudium et Spes* #45:1)

The Church is not like any human club or association. As mystery, it is both visible and spiritual, both active and contemplative, *both human and divine*. (CCC #771, with reference to *Sacrosanctum Concilium* #2) United to Christ, the Church is sanctified by him. It is a matter of faith that the Church is seen as "unfailingly holy." (CCC #823) And yet, as is often so painfully clear, members of the Church are sinners, always in need of purification. For the Church's members, "perfect holiness is something yet to be acquired." (CCC #825, citing *Lumen Gentium* #48:3)

We must bear this truth in mind whenever we hear of the failures or sins of any members of the Church, especially those in positions of leadership today. Whatever the faults or sins of any member of the Church, we can take great comfort in knowing that Christ (and his Spirit) will never abandon the Church, which is Christ's own "body." (Of course, when members of the Church sin, the harm done – and the scandal created – is that much worse precisely because they are members of Christ's own body.)

Why is the Church often called the "body of Christ"? A document from the Second Vatican Council, *Lumen Gentium*, explains: "By communicating his Spirit, Christ mystically constitutes as his body those brothers of his who are called together from every nation." (#7) Christ is the head of this body.

As members of Christ's body, each of us is also united *with each other* in Christ. But such unity does not mean there cannot be diversity at the same time:

Life in Christ

In the building up of Christ's Body there is engaged a diversity of members and functions. There is only one Spirit who, according to his own richness and the needs of the ministries, gives his different gifts for the welfare of the Church. (CCC #791, citing *Lumen Gentium* #7.3)

The "people of God" is made up of the hierarchy, lay people, and those in consecrated life (priests and religious). In other words, all of us! Lay people (many of whom are married) have a special task: to "seek the kingdom of God by engaging in temporal affairs by ordering them according to the plan of God." (*Lumen Gentium* #31) As we will see, each member of the body of Christ has a unique and necessary role to play in building the kingdom of God.

The Church is also often called the "Bride of Christ," a name that is especially significant for our purposes. Marriage has always been understood as the uniting of two persons, bride and groom, in the closest personal relationship. The unity of Christ and his Church has a similar intimate nature. In fact, Christ refers to himself as the "bridegroom." (Mark 2:19) And as St. Paul says, "Husbands, love your wives, just as Christ loved the church and gave himself up for her, in order to make her holy ...." (Ephesians 5:25-26)

In the Book of Revelation, the last book of the Bible, the Church is presented as the spotless bride of the spotless Lamb, the risen and glorious Christ. As Revelation 19.7 says, "Let us rejoice and exult ... for the marriage of the Lamb has come, and his bride has made herself ready." What is the heavenly "marriage of the Lamb"? It will be the complete and eternal union of Christ with his Bride, the Church, and all her members.[2] And most fittingly, we are told that there will be a "heavenly banquet" in celebration of this glorious union. We have received an invitation – to enjoy the baptismal gift of eternal life: "Blessed are those who are invited to the marriage supper of the Lamb." (Revelation 19:9)

When we talk about the Church, we should also consider its teaching authority, or the Magisterium. How can we, the people of God through the ages, be sure that the faith given to us is the same as the one that was handed on by the Apostles? How can unity among the members of the Body of Christ be maintained? How can we know that the Gospel has not been changed by human bias or prejudice? We know because, as we have seen, Christ sent us his Spirit to teach and remind us. Here is what the *Catechism* says about the Magisterium: "To fulfill this service, Christ endowed the Church's shepherds with the charism of infallibility in matters of faith and morals. The exercise of this charism takes several forms ...." (CCC #890)

The exercise of this teaching authority in the Church is *always* a participation in Christ's own authority and truth. It is done in service of Revelation, seeking only to hand on faithfully what has been received. This means that a teaching about a certain action, such as abortion, is not true simply because the Pope and bishops say so; rather, they say so because such an action is radically opposed to what Christ teaches about true love of God and neighbour. How could it be otherwise? Many people think that the Church should revise – if not throw out – some of its core teachings, especially in the area of life issues and sexuality. But when a certain teaching has been consistently and universally presented, this is because it is understood to fall within the "logic of gospel love." It is consistent with the truth of who we are. Those who have teaching authority in the Church are not free to revise or reject any clearly defined teachings, even when there is enormous public pressure to do so.

This brief introduction to the Church would be incomplete if we did not mention Mary. As the mother of Christ, she is also the mother of his Church. This means she is our mother, too. That is why she has various titles, including "Advocate, Helper, Benefactress, and Mediatrix." (CCC #969, citing *Lumen Gentium* #62)

Baptism: Putting on Christ

Baptism is one of the seven sacraments. The other six are confirmation, Eucharist, penance (reconciliation), anointing of the sick, holy orders – and, of course, matrimony! (CCC #1210) Sacraments are those "perceptible signs (words and actions) accessible to our human nature. By the action of Christ and the power of the Holy Spirit they make present ... the grace that they signify." (CCC #1084)

As the basis of the whole of Christian life, baptism is the "gateway" to life in the Spirit. (CCC #1213) As St. Paul explains,

Do you not know that all of us who have been baptized into Christ Jesus were baptized into his death? We were buried therefore with him by baptism into death, so that as Christ was raised from the dead by the glory of the Father, we too might walk in newness of life. (Romans 6:3-4)

The essential rite of baptism involves pouring water over the candidate's head (or immersing him or her in water) while invoking the Most Holy Trinity: the Father, the Son and the Holy Spirit. (CCC #1278) While faith is required for baptism, this faith is obviously not perfect or mature, but only a "beginning." (CCC #1253)

Immersion in water is a sign not only of death and purification, but also of rebirth. In receiving the gift of the Holy Spirit, the baptized receive sanctifying grace (the grace of "justification"), which restores them to right relationship with God. Sins (original sin and personal sins) are forgiven — so they can partake in the life of the Trinity. But as we saw in Chapter 1, the inclination to sin caused by the wounding of our nature remains. The baptized have "put on Christ" and are "configured" to him, marked with an "indelible spiritual mark" or the "seal" of the Lord; they are a "new creation," and have been incorporated in the body of Christ, the Church. (CCC #1262–1274)

Is baptism really necessary in our world today? The Church teaches that baptism is indeed necessary for the salvation of those to whom the Gospel has been proclaimed and who can ask for it. As the *Catechism* explains, "The Church does not know of any means other than Baptism that assures entry into eternal beatitude; this is why she takes care not to neglect the mission she has received from the Lord to see that all who can be baptized are reborn of water and the Spirit." (CCC #1257)

The *Catechism* goes on to say, "God has bound salvation to the sacrament of Baptism, but he himself is not bound by his sacraments." (CCC #1257) That means while we are always called to witness to Christ, to be "living invitations to him," is not for us to set limits on God's grace and mercy and desire that all will be saved. God is in charge!

You may have heard that "Outside the Church, there is no salvation." To put this teaching in positive terms, this means, as we have seen, that "all salvation comes from Christ the Head through the Church which is his Body." (CCC #846) But what about people who do not know Christ and his Church? The Vatican II Document *Ad Gentes* explains, "... in ways known to himself God can lead those who, through no fault of their own, are ignorant of the Gospel, to that faith without which it is impossible to please him ...." (CCC #848, citing *Ad Gentes* #7) Even so, the Church maintains that it is her mission to evangelize all men and women; and if the gospel is truly the good news it claims to be, wouldn't it be strange *not* to want to share it? However, for Christians, such sharing must always be a matter of proposing – and never imposing – the Gospel.

Our Vocation in Christ:
Making a commitment to love

Faith in Christ is not just an idea. It is a way of being. What does it mean in a tangible sense for us to become "partakers of the divine nature" through baptism? Christ himself provides the answer.

As the Vatican II document *Gaudium et Spes* states, "Christ ... makes man fully manifest to himself and brings to light his exalted vocation." (#22) The document offers more guidance, noting that man "cannot fully find himself except though a sincere gift of self." (#24) In making such a gift of self, we most clearly imitate Christ's own example.

One contemporary theologian gives thought-provoking commentary on what it means to become increasingly Christlike. Commenting on *Veritatis Splendor*, the 1993 papal encyclical on the foundations of the Christian moral life, J.A. DiNoia observes that it can be easy for Christians to lose sight of (or take for granted) the "stunning truth of the destiny" to which we have been called, "a truth proclaimed by Christ and made possible by his passion, death and resurrection." As DiNoia reminds us, our faith teaches that "the triune God could not bring about a more intimate union with created persons than that which has begun in Baptism and is to be consummated in the life to come" (at the "wedding feast" of the Lamb).³

DiNoia writes,
If we are destined to enjoy ultimate communion with the Father, Son and Holy Spirit – and with each other in them

– then we must change. We must be transformed into the people who can enjoy this destiny ... this transformation will be a conformation: the more we become like Christ, the more surely do we discover our true selves.[4]

Seen in this light, the moral life is our response to the love of God, a willingness to cooperate with the grace he has offered. It is a matter of commitment to love. Our daily choices matter so much because they shape us to be certain kinds of people, for better or for worse. We can become people with bigger hearts and a greater capacity to love – or not. We are free to respond to God's invitation (and grace) and grow into deeper union with God. Or, we can reject his invitation through the choices we make. It is no secret that the moral teachings of the Church are sometimes seen as a list of "no"s – of rules set by those in authority to keep us from having fun. Such a legalistic understanding could not be further from the truth. The Church's rules are not random, but aim to protect true human goods and help us to become good also. They exist to guide our freedom in choosing well. A key part of today's "new evangelization" is appreciating that good moral teaching must explain why certain "rules" exist. "Just because" is not a satisfactory answer!

As we will see in Chapter 4, married people have countless opportunities each day to make choices that will help them to become the kind of people who will enjoy their ultimate destiny. There are many moments when we can ask ourselves, "Who am I becoming?" It is not surprising that marriage (through which many people do a lot of their "becoming") has been called a little school of love.

It is true that each person makes his or her own gift of self through one state in life or another. We often hear about the vocation to the priesthood, to religious life, to marriage and sometimes to the single state. But vocation means much more.

In recent years, the ancient idea that each of us also has a unique personal vocation has resurfaced. The authors of *Personal Vocation: God Calls Everyone by Name* explain that a personal vocation is not just the calling to make a single commitment – to marriage, consecrated life or ordained ministry. As they put it,

... being followers of Jesus does not make us his clones ... Instead, each of us has something else important to do. Each has a particular set of gifts, opportunities, and other attributes – including weaknesses and strengths – that is uniquely our own. And each of us is obliged to examine that package to determine its potential for communicating God's love and truth, confronting evil (including the evil in ourselves) ... In this way we discover our personal vocations, the particular ways God calls us as unique individuals to help meet the needs of the Church and the world, and cooperate with him in redemption.[5]

Whether you are thinking about getting engaged, or are already engaged and are preparing for marriage, this is a perfect time to do some personal discernment. What are your gifts? What are your weaknesses and challenges? What unique path of love has God called you to follow? And if it seems that it is God's will that you marry your partner, what will God ask of you as a couple married "in the Lord"?

In the next chapter, we'll find out what it means to be married "in the Lord."

3

Marriage "in the Lord": What's Different About Christian Marriage?

Obviously, Christians are not the only people who get married. Nor do Christians have a monopoly on love! We all know wonderful people of other faiths, or people who have no explicit religious faith, who have happy and loving marriages and families that contribute much to society. No surprise there. The mutual attraction and complementarity between women and men, which makes it possible for them to bond in a unique way and transmit human life, is a natural, created reality. As the *Catechism* says, "The vocation to marriage is written in the very nature of man and woman as they come from the hand of the Creator." (CCC #1603) This means that marriage is not a purely "human" institution or construct. God is its author.

Almost all societies over the millennia have seen marriage as a great good. They have celebrated it and supported it in various ways. (However, the dignity of the institution has not been recognized at all times and in all places.) Even today, most people would agree that the healthy functioning of individuals (especially children) and of society itself depends on the well-being and stability of marriages. Again, you don't have to be religious to agree that this is so.

If all members of the human family experience the wounding of human nature (as a result of our first parents' original sin, as we saw in Chapter 1), it stands to reason that all marriages are also vulnerable to the effects of sin. These include discord, attempts to dominate, infidelity, jealousy, resentments, and much more. (CCC #1606)

But in positive terms, marriage and family life often help (or perhaps force!) people to get over themselves — to overcome selfishness and immaturity.

So what, if anything, is different about marriage "in the Lord"? What makes it a sacrament? We find a general answer in all that has been said so far in this book. Because of his or her baptism, the Christian is a "new creation" (Galatians 6:15; 2 Corinthians 5:17), healed of sin and a partaker in the divine nature. Since Christians have been transformed from within, a marriage between Christians will similarly be transformed "from within."

People sometimes wonder why the Church is so "controlling" about marriage. Why must it set the terms of who is eligible for marriage in the Church and even what must happen during the wedding ceremony itself? By now, the answer should be clear: the baptized belong to Christ and his Church. All that they are (and do) affects the rest of Christ's body. So the marriage of those who live "in the Lord" can never be just a private matter. It is already a Church matter. And it is also an occasion of joy for all members of Christ's body.

What does the New Testament say?

Let's look at a few key passages on marriage in the New Testament. Since actions speak louder than words, Christ's presence at the wedding feast at Cana is very significant. Mary, Jesus and his disciples had been invited to a wedding. When the wine ran out, Mary told Jesus. He then told the servants to fill some empty jars with water. When they had done so, Jesus said to take some of the liquid to the steward to taste. The steward tasted the water that had become wine, but did not know where it had come from. He called the bridegroom and said, "Everyone serves the good wine first, and then the inferior wine after the guests have become drunk. But you have kept the good wine until now." (John 2:1-11)

This was the first of Jesus' public signs. As we will see, just as he was present and effective at the wedding at Cana, he is present and effective in the marriages of all his followers. The *Catechism* says that this story shows "the confirmation of the goodness of marriage and the proclamation that henceforth marriage will be an efficacious sign of Christ's presence." (CCC #1613)

What did Jesus actually say about marriage? The Gospel of Matthew tells of an encounter between Jesus and the Pharisees. Under the old law of Moses, men were allowed to divorce their wives. So the Pharisees had asked Jesus if he agreed it was lawful to divorce one's wife for any cause. He replied,

> Have you not read that the one who made them at the beginning "made them male and female" [Genesis 1:27] and said, "for this reason a man shall leave his father and mother and be joined to his wife, and the two shall become one flesh"? [Genesis 2:24] So they are no longer two, but one flesh. Therefore what God has joined together, let no one separate. (Matthew 19:4-7)

When pressed further to explain why Moses allowed divorce, Jesus responded, "It was because you were so hard-hearted that Moses allowed you to divorce your wives, but from the beginning it was not so." (Matthew 19:8; see also Mark 10:2-12 and Luke 16:18) (Being "hard-hearted" today could be a matter of being resentful, of holding grudges.) Jesus' first response makes a clear reference to the creation accounts in Genesis, which we looked at in Chapter 1. In doing so, Jesus reaffirms the goodness of human sexuality and marriage as created realities – and Jesus reminds his listeners of God's original plan for human love, "in the beginning." As Jesus says, God himself has determined that marriage must not be dissolved; it is for life![6]

St. Paul's Letter to the Ephesians also helps us to understand marriage as a sacrament. Paul tells the people of Ephesus:

> Husbands, love your wives, just as Christ loved the Church and gave himself up for her, in order to make her holy by cleansing her with the washing of water by the word ... In the same way, husbands should love their wives as they do their own bodies. He who loves his wife loves himself. For no one ever hates his own body, but he nourishes and tenderly cares for it, just as Christ does for the Church, because we are members of his body. "For this reason a man will leave his father and mother ...." This is a great mystery, and I am applying it to Christ and the Church. (Ephesians 5:25-33)

This passage compares the love between husband and wife to the mystery of Christ and his Church. (In Chapter 2, we noted that Christ is presented as the "Bridegroom" of his beloved "bride," the Church.) In a thought-provoking Apostolic Letter, *Dignity and Vocation of Women*, Pope John Paul II comments that comparing the Church's relationship to Christ with that of a husband and wife moves in two directions that make up the whole of the "great mystery." According to John Paul II, the covenant (marriage) of human spouses "explains" the spousal character of the union of Christ with the Church. At the same time, the union (or "great sacrament") of Christ and his Church sets marriage as a "holy covenant" between the man and woman. (#23)

Much lively debate has come from the lines before the above verses: "Wives, be subject to your husbands as you are to the Lord. For the husband is the head of the wife ...." (Ephesians 5:22) John Paul II acknowledges that Paul's way of speaking here is very much rooted in the customs and religious tradition of his time, when women's social roles were very different from what they are today. But in the context of new life in Christ, this way of speaking "is to be understood and carried out in a new way: as a *'mutual subjection out of reverence for Christ'*." (See also Ephesians 5:21.) For John Paul II, this "mutual subjection" is nothing short of a "gospel innovation" that is made possible by our redemption in Christ. (#24)

John Paul admits that living the gospel innovation will always require conversion. Sadly, we do not have to look far today to see that institutions, individuals and attitudes do not always fully respect women as persons. As in Jesus' day, sin continues to infect and distort relations between the sexes. At the same time, we can find examples of "reverse discrimination" in our society – denials of the unique value and contributions of men. Some women (and schools of thought) argue that men are inferior simply because they are men, and that all of the world's problems can be blamed on men. Again, as John Paul makes clear, the gospel innovation applies equally to women and men. Both spouses are to love and serve and defer to each other in Christ. Of course, this is easier said than done!

You may be thinking, is any of this really possible? The Pharisees (and many others) of Jesus' time were also skeptical. Today, marriages face pressures that simply didn't exist in first-century Judea. People are marrying later, but living longer. Most of us are often too busy to focus on the truly important things. In this era of Facebook and texting, raising children is more complicated than ever. Many couples have no community or family support systems nearby. And the list goes on. Is Christ simply out of touch? Is he asking more than even people who mean well can deliver?

Christ himself says "no." Yes, there is a cost to following him: "If any want to become my followers, let them deny themselves and take up their cross and follow me." (Mark 8:34) Luckily, Christ is always there to help us in our struggles.

Marriage as sacrament:
An intimate community of life and love

Presenting Christian marriage as a fruit of Christ's cross – the source of all Christian life – is the key to understanding its sacramental nature. (CCC #1615) As we have seen, the Holy Spirit spreads the grace of Christ throughout the Church using the signs and instruments we call sacraments. (CCC #774) How is marriage a distinctive sign and instrument of grace? In what follows, we will draw on some important Church documents to "unpack" what has been said so far.

Gaudium et Spes (the Vatican II document on the Church in the modern world) contains some of the most beautiful and important passages on marriage of recent decades. Marriage is described as an "intimate partnership of life and love"[7] rooted in a "conjugal covenant of irrevocable personal consent." The document goes on to say, "By their very nature, the institution of matrimony itself and conjugal love are ordained for the procreation and education of children, and find in them their ultimate crown." (#48)

Describing marriage as a covenant goes far beyond seeing it simply as a type of contract. (Although marriage does involve a contract, it is much more than that.) A contract is a financial or legal agreement made between two parties, before witnesses and involving property. If the contract is broken, there are material consequences, such as the loss of the pledged property. A covenant, on the other hand, is a transformative relationship. It involves promising one's very self to another.[8] Marriage involves such a pledge of self.

The above description is of a rich and multifaceted human reality. At the heart of the Catholic world view is the understanding that grace does not annihilate our human nature; rather, grace perfects our human nature by healing it and raising it to share in God's own life. So when two Christians marry, their true human love is not denied or replaced, but healed and perfected "from within." *Gaudium et Spes* goes on to explain that when Christians marry, their "authentic married love is caught up into divine love and is governed and enriched by Christ's redeeming power and the saving activity of the Church." (#48)

John Paul II also speaks of the way that human love is infused (or "interiorly transformed") with Christ's own love:

> ... the marriage of baptized persons thus becomes a real symbol of that new and eternal covenant sanctioned in the blood of Christ. The Spirit which the Lord pours forth gives a new heart, and renders man and woman capable of loving one another as Christ has loved us. Conjugal love reaches that fullness to which it is interiorly ordained, conjugal charity, which is the proper and specific way in which the spouses participate in and are called to live the very charity of Christ who gave himself on the Cross. (*Familiaris Consortio*, #13)

In other words, with new hearts, the spouses can truly love each other as Christ loved. They both participate in – and actually signify – the new covenant or marriage between Christ and his Church.

On their wedding day, the bride and groom are often visibly overcome with emotion. Their deep love for each other is for them one of life's greatest blessings. It is a cause of tremendous joy and gratitude. But there is even more to celebrate! When the love of bride and groom is infused with Christ's own love, the spouses also have a "foretaste" of the joy that we hope will be ours at the "heavenly banquet."

In Chapter 1 we saw that God is himself a communion of love between co-equal persons. We can now say that marriage – as the communion of love between two distinct and equal persons – also reflects (in its own finite way) something of the life of the Triune God.

Marriage "in the Lord"

The *Catechism* summarizes much of the above in its opening paragraph on the sacrament of marriage:

> The matrimonial covenant, by which a man and woman establish between themselves a partnership of the whole of life, is by its nature ordered toward the good of the spouses and the procreation and education of offspring; this covenant between baptized persons has been raised by Christ the Lord to the dignity of a sacrament. (CCC #1601, citing *Code of Canon Law* #1055)

In what follows, we will focus on several aspects of marriage that the *Catechism* explores: the celebration of marriage; matrimonial consent; the effects of the sacrament of matrimony; and the goods and requirements of conjugal love. (Our concern is primarily with marriage as it is celebrated in the Latin Rite, rather than the Eastern Rites, which Ukrainian Catholics and others follow.[9]) While what follows is somewhat technical at times, I hope the information will be of use.

A sacramental marriage is between two validly baptized Christians. This is the case if both parties are Catholic, if neither is a Catholic, or if one is Catholic and the other is Orthodox or Protestant. The marriage of Catholics (even if only one party is Catholic) is governed by canon (Church) law, in addition to the divine law. (*Code of Canon Law* 1059) A marriage between a Catholic and baptized non-Catholic is sometimes referred to as a "mixed" marriage. By focusing on their common faith in Christ, spouses can learn from each other and can contribute to healing the wounds of the separation among Christians. However, their union also highlights the tragic fact that such separation still exists. As the *Catechism* cautions, such spouses "risk experiencing the tragedy of Christian disunity even in the heart of their own home." (CCC #1634) For liceity (legitimacy), Canon (church) law requires that a mixed marriage receive the "express permission" of Church authority. (CCC #1635, citing *Code of Canon Law* 1124)

A marriage between a Christian and someone who has not been baptized is not a sacrament, though it is still valid as a "natural marriage." The marriage between a Catholic and a non-baptized person is sometimes described as involving "disparity of cult." As we have seen,

Christians are not the only ones who hold marriage in high esteem and appreciate its importance for society. And to state the obvious, those who do not share faith in Christ often show us what it means to be a devoted spouse or parent or generous member of society. But, with much data to draw upon, the Church realistically observes that when the Christian faith is not shared by spouses, something very important is not shared. Tensions can arise, especially when it comes to decisions about raising children. The Christian spouse may even slip into a kind of "religious indifference" as a way to diffuse tensions. (CCC #1634) So when there is disparity of cult, an "express dispensation" is required for the marriage to be valid. (CCC #1635, citing *Code of Canon Law* 1086) When such permission is given, it is understood that both parties know and do not exclude the essential properties and ends of marriage. It is also presupposed that the Catholic has made known to the non-Catholic his or her own obligations: these include keeping his or Catholic faith and doing all in his or her power to baptize and raise their children as Catholics. (CCC #1635, citing *Code of Canon Law* 1125)

While there are real challenges when both spouses do not share the Christian faith, there is also opportunity, especially if the "Good News" is what it claims to be. The Christian husband or wife can become a compelling "living invitation" to Christ. As St. Paul wrote, "For the unbelieving husband is consecrated through his wife, and the unbelieving wife is consecrated through her husband." (CCC#1637, citing 1 Cor. 7:14)

The celebration of marriage

In the Latin Rite, the celebration of marriage between two Catholics usually takes place during the Eucharist, or Mass. In receiving the Eucharist together, the couple truly forms "one body" in Christ. (CCC #1621) What could be more appropriate or moving?

In the Latin tradition, the spouses act as ministers of Christ's grace. They confer the sacrament of matrimony on each other when they express their consent before the Church. (The priest doesn't marry you; he presides at the sacrament. You marry each other.)

In the Eastern Rite churches, the priest or bishop is a witness to the consent given by the spouses, but his blessing is also necessary for the sacrament to be valid. (CCC #1623)

Because marriage is an ecclesial act or community event, the priest or deacon who assists at the marriage celebration receives the consent of the spouses in the name of the Church and gives the Church's blessing. The presence of two witnesses also reflects the fact that the marriage is an ecclesial reality. For a marriage to be valid, the established ecclesiastical form for the celebration of marriage must be observed. Again, this is also the case even when only one of the baptized parties is Catholic. (*Code of Canon Law* 1108–1123)

Matrimonial consent

Some of the most memorable moments in wedding ceremonies occur when the bride and groom say their "I do"s.

The exchange of consent between the spouses is the element that makes the marriage. If there is no true consent, there is no marriage. (CCC #1626, citing *Code of Canon Law* 1057) Consent is a human act of will "by which a man and woman mutually give and accept each other through an irrevocable covenant in order to establish marriage." (*Code of Canon Law* 1057) No human power can substitute for it. (*Code of Canon Law* 1057) The covenant established by consent is fulfilled in their becoming "one flesh." (We will consider "consummation" below.)

There can be no marriage if either party is bound by an impediment in any natural or Church law. Impediments hinder one's freedom to offer oneself completely. If one party is married to someone else or is in sacred orders (a priest), or bound by a perpetual vow of chastity (as a religious brother or sister), these are examples of impediments to marriage. (*Code of Canon Law* 1083–1094)

Valid sacramental consent requires, among other things, that both parties have the necessary capacity to make a truly free choice for marriage and assume its obligations; they are "at least not ignorant" of the basic meaning and purposes of marriage; there is no deceit, force or fear and their consent is unconditional (that is, free from some future condition being placed on the marriage). Finally, the "internal assent of the mind" must be in keeping with the words and signs of consent. In other words, you have to mean what you are saying. (*Code of Canon Law* 1095–1107)

When the bride and groom make their vows, what are they agreeing to?

Let's consider what they actually do and say on the big day. In the Rite of Catholic Marriage, the wedding vows are usually preceded by three questions from the priest (or deacon):

(Name) and (name), have you come here freely and without reservation to give yourselves to each other in marriage?

Will you honour each other as man and wife for the rest of your lives?

Will you accept children lovingly from God, and bring them up according to the law of Christ and his Church?

If both answer "yes" or "I will," the priest (or deacon) then says, "Since it is your intention to enter into marriage, join your right hands, and declare your consent before God and his Church."

The moment everyone has been waiting for has finally arrived. The groom pledges: "I (name), take you (name), to be my wife. I promise to be true to you in good times and in bad, in sickness and in health. I will love you and honour you all the days of my life." And then the bride does the same! Is it any wonder that there are often lots of tears of joy?

Many wedding guests often say that a couple's exchange of vows reminded them of their own wedding day and the promises they made. The bride's and groom's dedication, courage and faith (in each other and in God) can inspire other couples to recommit to trying to love as Christ loves.

The priest acknowledges that the two have declared their consent to be married; he prays for God's blessing on them and proclaims, "What God has joined, men must not divide." The man and woman have become husband and wife. The declaration of consent is followed by the blessing of the rings.[10]

The words of consent make a marriage that is valid and "ratified" before God. But marriage is a union of embodied persons, not

Marriage "in the Lord"

just their minds. Consummation (sexual intercourse, or the "marital embrace" or "conjugal act") is the bodily expression of the mutual, total and unconditional gift of self that was made in the words of consent. In the act of consummation, each spouse also says to the other: Without reservation, I give all that I am to you – and I accept you, even with your imperfections. (And isn't this how Christ loves each of us?) When a marriage is both ratified and consummated, the natural bond is perfected and cannot be dissolved by any human power. (*Code of Canon Law* 1141)

Civil law of the provinces and territories of Canada recognizes a religious celebration of marriage. Couples give their consent only once, but they must obtain a marriage license from their province or territory before the ceremony. This license guarantees, among other things, that neither party is already married. After the wedding at the church, the marriage must be registered with the provincial or territorial registry office.

What if someone seeking marriage in the Church explicitly and formally rejects what the Church intends to do when the marriage of baptized persons is celebrated? In such a case, the obstacle to marriage is not raised by the Church, but by the person (or couple) seeking marriage in the Church. (*Familiaris Consortio* #68) In effect, the person is asking for something and yet rejecting that very thing at the same time. In such a situation, the person must try to be honest about what he or she really wants. This can be a great opportunity to explore one's faith – or the reasons why one may have rejected faith. True spiritual growth can come from this kind of reflection.

The effects of the sacrament

As Pope John Paul II explains, "… the first and immediate effect of marriage (*res et sacramentum*) is not supernatural grace itself, but the Christian conjugal bond, a typically Christian communion of two persons because it represents the mystery of Christ's incarnation and the mystery of his covenant." (*Familiaris Consortio* #13) This is why we often refer to spouses as a "couple." As a participation in the great mystery of Christ's own sacrificial love, the bond created is a truly supernatural bond – and a gift from God. As one contemporary writer explains, "the Spirit of unity effects the bond, his objective consecration wrought through the spouses in their consent and consummation."[11] The bond therefore is not a thing, but a permanent union and communion of two persons.[12] (That's why marriage is different from simply living together.)

On the basis of this bond, the Spirit of Christ's love is poured into the hearts of the spouses precisely in their lived "intimate community of life and love." What are the graces of the sacrament? As *Gaudium et Spes* observes,

> ... Christian spouses have a special sacrament by which they are fortified and receive a kind of consecration in the duties and dignity of their state. By virtue of this sacrament, as spouses fulfill their conjugal and family obligation, they are penetrated with the Spirit of Christ, which suffuses their whole lives with faith, hope and charity. Thus they increasingly advance the perfection of their own personalities, as well as their mutual sanctification, and hence contribute jointly to the glory of God. (#48)

The grace proper to the sacrament of marriage strengthens the couple's love and unity. (In Chapter 5 we'll say more about the nature of the special gifts or graces that spouses receive.)

The goods and requirements of conjugal love

The Church has traditionally identified specific "goods" of marriage. The *Catechism* says,

> Conjugal love involves a totality, in which all the elements of the person enter ... it aims at a deeply personal unity, a unity that, beyond union in one flesh, leads to forming one heart and one soul; it demands *indissolubility* and *faithfulness* in definitive mutual giving, and it is open to *fertility*. (CCC #1643, citing *Familiaris Consortio* #13)

It is the very nature of married love to require *unity* and *indissolubility* (cannot be dissolved or ended). How could it be otherwise? The spouses have formed a "union of two" that embraces their entire life. They are called to grow in their communion. To speak of the indissolubility of sacramental marriage is to acknowledge that the marriage bond is an abiding reality and a gift of the Spirit. Even though the bond is unbreakable, each person remains distinct. Marriage is not a "fusion" of two moral agents, but a "communion of two."[13] Interestingly, it is precisely through the permanent mutual gift of self that spouses often become more fully themselves. As we have seen, we are made for love – to give and receive it. Most people would say that knowing they are loved unconditionally helps them to grow as a person and in freedom. In an age that prizes personal freedom above all, it is worthwhile to keep this point in mind!

Conjugal love also requires an "inviolable fidelity" (faithfulness) from each spouse. This also is the natural consequence of the gift of themselves. As the *Catechism* observes, "Love seeks to be definitive; it cannot be an arrangement 'until further notice.'" (CCC #1646)

Of course, the deepest reason for fidelity and indissolubility of marriage is found in the relationship between Christ and his Church. Christ's love for and bond to his Church are unbreakable. Spouses whose love shares in and symbolizes Christ's love are similarly joined by an unbreakable bond. (CCC #1647) In this light, the seriousness of adultery and the heartache associated with it are impossible to deny.

Openness to fertility is one of the other "goods and requirements of conjugal love." We will look at this topic in the next chapter as we explore the real-life and everyday implications of marriage "in the Lord." We will also consider the fourth "good" of marriage, the "good of the spouses."

4

Sacramental Marriage: How Do We Live It?

It is one thing to talk about marriage as a sacrament, but quite another matter to live it, day in and day out. In this chapter we will look at what marriage "in the Lord" means in practical terms for couples today. Think of it as a move from dusty theology textbooks to the trenches of real life.

As the introductory paragraph on marriage in the *Catechism of the Catholic Church* says, marriage has two overarching ends or purposes: "the good of the spouses" and the "procreation and education" of children. (CCC #1601) As we have just seen, these are also described as "goods" of marriage. Let's explore each of the two purposes of marriage to find out how they are linked to each other.

The good of the spouses

On the wedding day, everyone wishes the bride and groom many years of happiness, children, fulfillment, health, prosperity, and other good things. As husband and wife, the couple will journey through life as best friends, as a team. They will "render mutual help and service to each other through an intimate union of their persons and their actions." (*Gaudium et Spes* #48) The wedding guests hope that this new couple will grow in their love for each other and in their experience of unity – and that someday, they will be that elderly couple out on the dance floor who have perfected the art of dancing together.

But in living a sacramental marriage, "the good of the spouses" means even more than this. As we saw in Chapter 2, if we are to fulfill our true vocation, we must become more like Christ, continually stretching our capacity to make a gift of self. To do this, we need all the help and practice we can get. Marriage is a blessing, in and of itself. For many people, it is also a lifelong school of learning to love as Christ loves. (This is what it means to be holy.)

That is why many people today would agree that the "good of the spouses" includes their growth in holiness in and through their married life. (As children in Grade 5 might say, it's about helping each other get to heaven.[14]) As the Fathers of the Second Vatican Council wrote, spouses "increasingly advance the perfection of their own personalities, as well as their mutual sanctification, and hence contribute jointly to the glory of God." (*Gaudium et Spes* #48)

This was hardly a new teaching at the time. In 1930, Pope Pius XI observed that married love includes the "mutual help" of the spouses. However, its ultimate purpose is this: that through their partnership, husband and wife should help each other to grow in virtue and, above all, in love of God and neighbour. (*Casti Connubii*, #23)

So how do spouses help each other to grow in virtue and in holiness in the 21st century? There is no specific list to follow, but this growth certainly involves giving and receiving encouragement, support, forgiveness and unconditional love. Spouses must also be honest and courageous and hold onto their sense of humour. Most importantly, in a world of countless demands and distractions, "the good of the spouses" is a matter of keeping each other focused on the things that really matter – and reminding each other of their call to follow Christ. (As one friend likes to say to her husband, "What have you done for my soul lately?") In this way, each spouse lives out his or her unique personal vocation and helps his or her partner to do the same.

The fruitfulness of love and the gift of children

One way to learn how to love as Christ loves – and to help your spouse do the same – is to become parents. Even couples who are trying to soothe a fussy newborn or deal with a hormone-driven teenager will say that being a parent is wonderful and rewarding. They will probably also admit that parenting often calls you to make sacrifices, which means growing in virtue. That is why the Church calls the family a "kind of school of deeper humanity." (*Gaudium et Spes* #52)

The Church does not deny the very real challenges parents face today. But it believes that in spite of the risks and concerns, children are the gift the world needs most. The Church reminds us that children are "the supreme gift of marriage." (*Gaudium et Spes* #50) They bring love and joy to the lives of everyone they touch, especially their parents. Children give life more meaning – at times, they even help their parents to grow up and act responsibly. The exuberance and spontaneity of children pull us out of our routines and remind us that we are not the masters of the universe. Children make life fun, even in the midst of chaos.

The Church describes marriage as "an intimate community of life and love" because love and life are deeply connected. God himself reflects this fundamental truth. God is a communion of "co-equal persons" who give themselves to each other in an exchange of love – and God is overwhelmingly life-giving! As the creation stories of the Book of Genesis tell us, God created everything (including us) not because he had to, but to express his love and goodness. (CCC #293) God called the first man and woman (and the rest of us) into existence *through* his love, and called them (and us) at the same time *for* love. (*Familiaris Consortio* #11)

It is the very nature of love to go beyond its own interests, to be creative, to be generous. Love energizes and inspires. Love is fruitful. Love is always known by the effects it has: for example, when we take care of a family member or friend who is sick, we find we have more stamina than we thought. Blessed Mother Teresa's love of God and neighbour gave her focus and energy that were the envy of people half her age. All of us – and again, not just Christians – have seen and felt the "inner dynamism" of love.

The love of spouses is also fruitful or life-giving – and often in its own unique way. Pope John Paul II speaks of the inner dynamism of love between spouses:

> In its most profound reality, love is essentially a gift; and conjugal love, while leading the spouses to the reciprocal "knowledge" which makes them "one flesh" (Gen. 2:24) does not end with the couple, because it makes them capable of the greatest possible gift, the gift by which they become

cooperators with God for giving life to a new human person. (*Familiaris Consortio* #14)

This is why love between spouses is often called both "unitive" (it bonds them) and "procreative" (it is life-giving). A child is not something added on to the couple's mutual gift from the outside. Rather, the child "springs from the very heart of that mutual giving, as its fruit and fulfillment." (CCC #2366) How fitting it is that when a husband and wife make a complete gift of self to each other, the symbol and sign of their gift is sometimes a new human person – someone who was also created *through* love and *for* love and relationship.

Sex has a transcendent meaning – it goes far beyond the physical act. Just as fidelity in marriage reflects Christ's fidelity to the Church, when married love is fruitful, it provides yet another type of reflection of the life and love of the Trinity. As the *Catechism* puts is, in the procreation and education of children, the family "reflects the Father's work of creation." (CCC #2205)

So it should come as no surprise that God's first command to Adam and Eve was to "be fruitful and multiply." During the wedding ceremony, when the bride and groom agree to "lovingly accept children," they are saying that they will allow their love to be true to its transcendent nature: generous and fruitful.

What a stunning privilege – and responsibility – the transmission of human life is. We often speak of "making babies," but in fact parents are *sharers* in God's creative power; they are the "interpreters" of the love of the Creator. (*Gaudium et Spes* #50) Parents provide "matter," but it is God who infuses an eternal soul as he bestows the gift of a new person. Children are gifts, not objects or "products" to be designed. By definition, a gift cannot be demanded.

Of course, the fruitfulness of conjugal love does not end with the conception of a new member of the human family. Fruitfulness also means ensuring that children are well cared for and receive a decent education and formation, especially in the moral and spiritual life.

Couples who do not have children are also called to be fruitful. As we know, infertility is a source of unspeakable heartache for many couples today. A Church that is so enthusiastically on the side of life must be sensitive to these couples. From our limited viewpoint, the situation does seem very unfair. Still, couples who are infertile also form a distinctive "communion of persons." Their love can be spiritually fruitful. Everyone knows wonderful couples whose love is expressed in many profound – and often surprising – ways. This is also the case for couples who marry after their child-bearing years are over.

The love between spouses (and the family's love) may also be expressed through welcoming others, making countless types of sacrifices, and serving those in need. It is the nature of love to overflow in all kinds of amazing ways. Pope John Paul II says that the "mission" of the family is "to guard, reveal and communicate love, and this is a living reflection of and a real sharing in God's love for humanity and the love of Christ the Lord for the Church His Bride." (*Familiaris Consortio* #17)

Making decisions together

Before and after marriage, couples must make decisions about when and how to express their love in an intimate physical way. What does the Church say?

What does it mean to be human?

To do justice to some of the most common questions in this area, we need to recall (from Chapter 1) that the human person is made of a body and a soul (or spirit). Many people today seem to think that it is the mind – and its ability to think and choose – that defines us. This view of the person sees the body as sub-human, as raw material for us to use or remake as we see fit. This is a dangerous idea that can lead us to ignore or disconnect from our bodies.

Pope John Paul II noticed that many people were starting to see their bodies as being separate from their minds. He knew that if they did this, they wouldn't be able to appreciate the truth and beauty of the Church's teaching on the meaning and purpose of human sexuality.

To address this problem, he gave a series of talks between 1979 and 1984 to present a complete view of the human person and human love in the divine plan. These talks have come to be known as the "theology of the body." A new translation has been published as *Man and Woman He Created Them: A Theology of the Body*.[15]

At the heart of Pope John Paul II's theology of the body is the idea that "... by means of its visible masculinity and femininity, the body, and it alone, is capable of making visible what is invisible: the spiritual and the divine."[16] The body reveals the person. Elsewhere, John Paul II said this about the role of the body in human love:

> As an incarnate spirit, that is a soul which expresses itself in a body and a body informed by an immortal spirit, man is called to love in a unified totality. Love includes the human body, and the body is made a sharer in spiritual love. (*Familiaris Consortio* #11)

The physical expression of spousal love

In other words, sexual intercourse is never just physical. The *Catechism* develops this point:

> ... sexuality, by means of which a man and woman give themselves to one another through acts which are proper and exclusive to spouses, is by no means something purely biological, but concerns the innermost being of the human person as such. It is realized in a truly human way only if it is an integral part of the love by which a man and a woman commit themselves totally to one another until death. (CCC #2361, citing *Familiaris Consortio* #11)

Sexual intercourse between spouses is "a sign and pledge of spiritual communion." (CCC #2360)

As we saw in Chapter 1, the body has a "spousal" meaning: the complementary design of men and women highlights the fact that we are created for relationship. In his theology of the body, Pope John Paul II says that the marital act speaks the "language of the body." Humans communicate in many ways, most often through words or gestures. (Whether someone is in Istanbul or Moose Jaw, a smile says that he or she is happy.) So what does sex between spouses say? As we saw earlier, consummating the marriage fulfills and expresses in a physical way the couple's consent to their marriage and all that it includes. The whole meaning of marriage – as an intimate community of life and love – is present and signified whenever the couple has intercourse.

The creation accounts in the Book of Genesis leave no doubt that the Bible affirms the goodness of the human body and human sexuality. To avoid confusion, the Catechism says,

> "The acts in marriage by which the intimate and chaste union of the spouses takes place are noble and honourable; the truly human performance of these acts fosters the self-giving they signify and enriches the spouses in joy and gratitude." Sexuality is a source of joy and pleasure. (CCC #2362, citing *Gaudium et Spes* #49)

Clearly, the Church is not "anti-body" or opposed to sex and pleasure! Just the opposite, in fact. It is because of its deep appreciation for the beauty, meaning and mystery of human sexuality that the Church treats matters relating to sexuality seriously and even reverently.

Still, each of us will be a work in progress until the day we die. Catholic moral teaching always reminds us that that we can have selfish desires and that they can be very strong in the area of our sexuality. We can start to idolize even things that are good in themselves, such as the physical expression of marital love. This is especially true in a culture that often seems obsessed with sex.

So while it sees sexuality as a good thing, the Church has a more honest – and ultimately liberating – message, especially for couples preparing for marriage. She reminds us that there are always profound goods at stake in physical intimacy. These ideas form the basis of the Church's teaching. Now let's look at three big questions that people often ask about: sex outside marriage, birth control, and reproductive technologies.

Why is the Church against sex outside marriage?

The Church's teaching on sex outside marriage follows from all that has been said so far about the meaning and purposes of human sexuality:

> The total physical self-giving would be a lie if it were not the sign and fruit of a total personal self-giving ... if the person were to withhold something or reserve the possibility of deciding otherwise in the future, by this very fact he or she would not be giving totally. (*Familiaris Consortio* #11)

Honesty is a universal human value: we should say what we mean and mean what we say. Sex outside marriage tries to "say" two contradictory things at the same time: on the one hand, I give my entire physical self to you; on the other hand, I have not made a total (exclusive and irrevocable) gift of myself to you. Even genuine love and the best of intentions (including having set a wedding date) cannot change this basic fact. With such a mixed message, how can there not be physical, emotional and spiritual consequences for both men and women – even if we deny that such consequences exist? Many hearts have been broken by unfulfilled expectations and empty promises.

The Church's "no" to sex outside marriage protects a much bigger "yes" to personal dignity and integrity. Such a teaching is anything but arbitrary. That is why the *Catechism of the Catholic Church* says fornication (sexual intercourse between two unmarried people) is "gravely contrary to the dignity of persons and of human sexuality ...." (CCC #2353) Scripture also condemns fornication as going against God's design for human sexuality (for example, see Exodus 20:14; Matthew 15:19, 19:18; Romans 13:9). A person who knows that fornication is wrong and yet freely chooses to engage in it anyway commits a serious sin.

Whenever the Church speaks of sin and the damage it causes, the Church also proclaims (with confidence and great joy) that God's love and mercy are greater than sin. We will have more to say about Christ's offer of reconciliation in the next chapter.

It is no secret that physical desire is a potent force, especially when two people truly love each other! But to love someone is also to be concerned for his or her spiritual well-being. The *Catechism* offers the following guidance for engaged couples:

> They should see in this time of testing a discovery of mutual respect, an apprenticeship in fidelity and the hope of receiving one another from God. They should reserve for marriage the

expressions of affection that belong to married love. They will help each other grow in chastity. (CCC #2350)

Chastity does not mean prudishness or fear about sex. It is part of the cardinal virtue (good habit) of temperance that moderates the attraction of pleasures and helps us use God's gifts in a healthy way. (CCC #1809) Chastity refers to the "successful integration of sexuality within the person and thus the inner unity of man is his bodily and spiritual being." (CCC #2337) All are called to live chastity in a way that is in keeping with their particular state in life. (CCC #2348) We all need chastity to be truly free and to flourish. Before we can make a true (conscious and free) gift of ourselves in marriage, we must first possess ourselves. (CCC #2339)

Marital chastity is not sexlessness in marriage. Rather, it is a genuine warmth that serves and reflects true intimacy. It involves fidelity, maturity and a healthy self-discipline.

What about birth control?

As we saw earlier, the Church teaches that the full meaning of marriage is signified and contained in each act of intercourse between spouses. The Pope's 1968 encyclical, *Humanae Vitae* ("On Human Life"), affirmed this teaching, saying that there is an "inseparable connection, established by God, which man on his own initiative may not break, between the unitive significance and procreative significance which are both inherent to the marriage act." (#12) This means that "each and every marriage act must remain open to the transmission of life." (#11)

But what does this mean for real people in the trenches of real life? Does the Church say that married couples must have as many children as they physically can? Are the unique (and sometimes very difficult) circumstances of a couple irrelevant when it comes to their decisions about family planning?

Humanae Vitae created a firestorm of debate when it was published in 1968, at the height of the sexual revolution. And yet, more than 40 years later, many Catholics have still not heard a positive – and coherent – presentation of the Church's teaching on the full truth about "responsible parenthood."

Sacramental Marriage

Humanae Vitae is a reflection on the nature of married love – especially the sacramental love between Christian spouses. Married love is *fully human and free;* it is *total;* it is also *faithful and exclusive* of all others until death; and married love is *fecund* or fruitful. (*Humanae Vitae* #9)

These are also characteristics of Christ's love for the Church, which should come as no surprise, since Christian spouses share in and try to model Christ's own love. They are called to love with all they have, and "to the end," as Christ did. Everything else that the encyclical says flows from this view of marriage.

It is possible to deny either the unitive or procreative meaning of sex in marriage. As *Humanae Vitae* observes, "a conjugal act imposed on one's partner without regard to his or her condition or reasonable wishes in the matter is no true act of love, and therefore offends the moral order ...." (#13) Something that is not a true act of love can never be unitive for the spouses. To love as Christ loves means that each spouse puts the other first, staying attentive to the other's needs and well-being (physical, emotional and spiritual).

When people use contraception, they are deliberately trying to prevent the procreative consequences of a freely chosen act of intercourse. (Contraception is something used before or during or after sex. This includes, among other things, the contraceptive pill, condoms, direct sterilization of the man or woman, and various forms of emergency contraception.) Contraception is therefore "objectively disordered" (wrong) in and of itself or "intrinsically evil." (CCC #2370, with reference to *Humanae Vitae* #14) As John Paul II explains,

> ... the innate language that expresses the total reciprocal self-giving of husband and wife is overlaid, through contraception, by an objectively contradictory language, namely that of not giving oneself totally to the other. This leads not only to a positive refusal to be open to life but also to a falsification of the inner truth of conjugal love, which is called to give itself in personal totality. (*Familiaris Consortio* #32)

Conjugal love can be diminished when the focus becomes self-gratification, for either person or even for both people. Separating the unitive and procreative aspects of sex makes the gift of procreation into a problem to be managed with technology. It turns it into something less than fully human. Contraception is essentially opposed to God's plan for marriage – for life and love. How can there *not* be negative consequences for the spouses – both as individuals and as a couple?

So what is a couple living in the modern world (with all its complexities and demands) to do? First, as spouses strive to grow together in virtue and holiness, they should regularly review their priorities, their existing duties to "God, themselves, their families and society." (*Humanae Vitae* #10) As they do this, they may legitimately decide that they have "well-grounded" (not selfish) reasons for spacing or postponing having children. Such reasons may be due to the "physical or psychological condition of husband or wife, or even from external circumstances." (*Humanae Vitae* #16) (They might include serious illness of husband or wife, existing obligations to a special needs child, or real financial hardship, etc.)

When there are serious reasons for avoiding pregnancy, couples still must respect God's design for human fertility and the objective moral order.

This does not mean you have to have 15 kids! There are ways to work with the woman's natural fertility cycles to postpone or try to achieve pregnancy. A healthy woman is fertile only for a limited number of days each month. (A healthy man is fertile all the time.) Women can learn to identify and interpret with great accuracy bodily signs that indicate fertile and infertile times. So contemporary methods of natural family planning[17] (NFP) are not the same as the old "rhythm method"! To postpone pregnancy (for a time or indefinitely), a couple abstains from intercourse when the woman's biological signs show that conception is possible. Contemporary methods of NFP, when used properly, are as effective as the types of artificial contraception (excluding complete sterilization).[18]

NFP is genuine family planning. Once the couple is aware of the woman's fertility cycle, they can have sex on fertile days once they are ready to welcome a child.[19]

Still, many people ask, if the aim or intention is the same – to avoid pregnancy when there are truly good reasons to do so – is there really a moral difference between various methods of contraception and NFP?

Sacramental Marriage

It is a basic principle of Catholic moral reasoning that, as important as good intentions are, the end does not justify the means. We have considered how the moral life is always a matter of growing in virtue or shrinking in vice. This means that *how* we achieve a desired end – the particular choices we make along the way – also matters.

It is true that NFP can be used for selfish reasons. But it can also be used for legitimate and moral reasons. It then reflects the understanding that "one is not the master of the sources of life but rather the minister of the design established by the Creator." (*Humanae Vitae* #13) Our society seems obsessed with technological manipulation of every aspect of life – even death. The practice of NFP reflects a very different attitude of wonder and "receptivity." It reminds us that we are only stewards of God's gifts and that we *collaborate* in the transmission of human life. NFP involves accepting the cycle of fertility, dialogue, mutual respect, shared responsibility and self-control. (*Familiaris Consortio* #32) In fact, NFP is more a lifestyle than a family planning "method."

Couples who practise NFP do not try to change the full meaning of the conjugal act. When they have sex, even during an infertile time, they offer all they have, by God's design. In this way they remain fully open to each other and "open to the transmission of life." This is also the case for those who are past child-bearing age or who are not able to conceive: even though their sexual union will not lead to a baby being conceived, the reason is outside their control. They, too, remain open to the transmission of life.

In a society that places a lot of value on personal freedom, efficiency, technological mastery of nature and sexual gratification, NFP is radically counter-cultural. There is no denying that it asks much of both husband and wife as they strive to grow in self-discipline and self-possession. At times it requires a sacrificial and even heroic love.

Thus, one key reason that the practice of NFP is morally good is that it helps spouses to grow in the virtue of conjugal chastity. And, as discussed above, chastity is essential for making a free and total gift of self. Moreover, as we saw in Chapter 2, in learning to love generously and give of self, we are striving to become more like Christ, who made the ultimate gift of self. We could therefore even say that NFP – especially when sacrifice is required – can help spouses to learn to love as Christ loves. If this is so, it is easier to understand why the Church is not in a position to "update" the teaching against contraception.

Couples use contraception when they want to avoid conception and also have sex on days when conception might otherwise occur. Many would accept that with such an approach, there is less need for communication, self-mastery and sacrifice, which are at the heart of the practice of NFP and conjugal chastity. Even though they may have truly noble intentions, couples who use contraception are – in effect – rejecting an important opportunity to grow in chastity and its related virtues. Contraception is not wrong because it is "unnatural" or "artificial" (after all, heart surgery and antibiotics are "artificial," too). As one contemporary theologian puts it, contraception is wrong "because it is essentially opposed to conjugal chastity and its requirement of a parentally responsible and virtuous bodily-sexual behavior."[20] Translation? It is wrong for all the reasons that NFP and periodic abstinence are good.

But it bears repeating: it is likely that many – if not a great majority – of couples have never heard the best of what the Church has to offer in its teaching about both contraception and responsible parenthood.

Still, the Church's teaching on responsible parenthood is an especially difficult one for most couples. And we live in a culture that makes it that much harder to live what is already a difficult teaching. So it is crucial to listen to the real-life experiences of couples who practise NFP. Many of them report the following: NFP has caused them to grow in respect for each other; it improves their communication (especially about the most important things); it calls for shared decision-making and shared responsibility for family planning. Couples report that periods of abstinence create a honeymoon effect when they start having sex again after a break. These may be some of the reasons why divorce rates among couples who practise NFP are startlingly low.[21]

It is also worth noting that understanding and tracking her fertility increases a woman's general health awareness. Unlike many forms of contraception, NFP is very low cost – and has no negative physical side effects for women.[22] It is also eco-friendly.

Forty years ago, *Humanae Vitae* predicted that the widespread use of contraceptives would have dire consequences for individuals and society as a whole. (#17)

We do not need to look far today to see that the great promises of the "sexual revolution" (which contraception helped to facilitate) have often failed to deliver. Are women that much happier today? Are men happier? Are marriages stronger? Is every child more loved? Does our culture have a healthy attitude towards sex? What messages regarding sex and commitment are young people hearing? There is now concern about the "demographic deficit" in affluent Western societies, where populations are shrinking. We can only wonder what role an increasingly anti-life or "contraceptive mentality" has played in this demographic shift.

While there are no easy answers to these very complex questions, perhaps there is enough personal and social data to suggest that although the teaching on responsible parenthood is challenging at times, it contains profound and timely wisdom about the nature of human life and love.

Can infertile Catholic couples use new reproductive technologies?

With the help of cutting edge medicine, many things are now possible. It is not surprising that many of the new reproductive technologies allow human life to be reproduced in a lab or clinic – without sex. But are all the advances in reproductive technologies necessarily a good thing? While contraception seeks sex without the possibility of a baby, some of the new reproductive technologies "produce" babies without sex.

The Church, which is enthusiastically pro-life, agrees that it is very good and natural for couples to want a child. Still, no one has the right to a child. Children are gifts to be received, not objects to be ordered.

As we said above, good intentions are not all that matters when it comes to moral choices, especially choices involving human life. We need to evaluate the means involved in the types of assisted reproduction available today to see if they respect the truth and innate dignity of human life and love. The Church offers criteria for evaluating reproductive technologies. Those interventions that *assist* the marital act in reaching its end of procreation (such as surgery to correct a blocked fallopian tube or the applications of NaProTECHNOLOGY to correct hormonal problems) can be morally good. Anything that *replaces* the marital act (such as in vitro fertilization or the use of donated eggs or sperm) cannot be morally good.[23]

This teaching helps to explain what is problematic about a procedure such as in vitro fertilization (IVF). Even though people may have the best intentions and much love to give to a child, it is beneath the dignity of any human to come into existence as the product of technical interventions by workers in a lab or clinic. As recent news reports tell us, children made in labs are increasingly subjected to quality control measures: the inferior are discarded. Also, in the process of IVF, more human beings are usually conceived (eggs fertilized or embryos produced) than can be implanted at once in a woman's uterus. The extra embryonic humans ("spare embryos") are typically frozen for an indefinite period of time. Still, all excess embryos are members of the human family. How is their absurd frozen existence in keeping with their human dignity?

Because of our tremendous dignity as creatures made in the image of God with a vocation to love, the only truly worthy context for a human life to be transmitted is the mutual and total self-gift of spouses in sexual intercourse, an act that is at the same time physical and spiritual. Anything else is truly "beneath our dignity."

There is a consistent logic and wisdom to the Church's teaching in this area, even when some aspects of this teaching are difficult to hear. In teaching always that marriage is an intimate communion of life and love, and that the unitive and procreative meanings of sexual intercourse between a husband and wife cannot be separated, the Church's only concern is to protect and promote the full truth about human life and love – and the dignity of all God's children.

5

Is Any of This Possible? Can We Really Love as Christ Loves?

You are not alone if, at this point, you find yourself saying, beautiful though it may be, is the vision of marriage and married life presented in this book beyond the reach of most people? That marriage can be a difficult business is not news. But most people would agree that new challenges today make it that much harder to succeed at marriage: the "pornification" of our culture has distorted attitudes and expectations about sex and true intimacy; the ever-rising cost of living – and of raising kids – adds to family stress levels; and there seems to be a growing pessimism (no longer just in Hollywood), about anyone's ability to be faithful to one person, and for life. Such widespread pessimism can be very demoralizing, especially during tough times.

The ongoing struggle of Christian life

The Christian life is an ongoing struggle to grow in holiness and to learn to love well. It is a struggle that is often experienced most acutely in marriage and family life.

But again, sin does not have the last word. The truly good news about marriage "in the Lord" is that the spouses don't have to rely solely on their own resources and skills to go the distance.

The grace of the sacrament

In Chapter 3, we saw that the first effect of marriage is the indissoluble (unbreakable) conjugal bond. This bond is a gift of the Holy

Spirit. It is precisely as "a typically Christian communion of two persons" (*Familiaris Consortio* #13) – as a couple – that spouses experience the specific graces of the sacrament of marriage.

As John Paul II explains, "The gift of Jesus is not exhausted in the actual celebration of the sacrament of marriage, but accompanies the married couple ...." (*Familiaris Consortio* #13) Through marriage, Christian spouses share – in a new way – in the mystery of the death and resurrection of Christ; their love is "purified and made holy." The sacrament "takes up and makes specific the sanctifying grace of Baptism." (*Familiaris Consortio* #56)

Obviously, this does not mean that there will be no heartaches or struggles in the couple's life. But it does mean that spouses don't have to face life's challenges on their own.

What does this look like in daily life? The grace of the sacrament heals disordered desires; it perfects the couple's love and strengthens their indissoluble unity. (CCC #1641) In other words,

> Christ dwells with them, gives them the strength to take up their crosses and follow him, to rise again after they have fallen, to forgive one another, to bear one another's burdens, to "be subject to one another out of reverence for Christ," (Eph. 5:21) and to love one another with supernatural, tender and fruitful love. (CCC #1642)

Of course, grace does not destroy human freedom! As one contemporary thinker puts it, God's constant offer of grace, which heals and elevates spouses, "is never separate from their cooperation, from their actions."[24] As long as spouses strive to live what the sacrament signifies, they can expect God to give them the help or graces they need, when they need them.[25]

Married couples can also experience the healing and transforming effects of the grace of the sacrament in the area of sexuality.

The grace of the sacrament helps spouses to love more authentically, more generously and more fully, if they so desire. But to state what is painfully obvious to pretty much everyone, growth in chastity is "a long and exacting work" – a work that is never fully accomplished in this life. Chastity has "laws of growth which progress through stages." (CCC #2343) As most people know from experience, the

Is Any of This Possible?

stages are often marked by imperfection and sin, and sometimes by disillusionment or despair with oneself. But remember, we are all works in progress.

The Church, as it encourages all individuals and couples, whatever their personal struggles, also reminds them of the need for "persistence and patience, humility and strength of mind, filial trust in God and in His grace, and frequent recourse to prayer and the sacraments of the Eucharist and Reconciliation." (*Familiaris Consortio* #33, with reference to *Humanae Vitae* #25) While the world often tells us to be totally self-sufficient, the Church has a different message.

When do we sin?

Fundamentally, sin is a matter of failure in relationship with God and with others. Many people today misunderstand the Church's teaching on sin. Let's take a brief look at this teaching.

A person sins when he or she understands that something is wrong (objectively disordered) and then freely chooses to do it anyway. In such a case, the person is morally responsible (culpable or blameworthy) for what was done.

But sometimes a person does something that is wrong in itself ("objectively disordered"), but does not know it to be wrong. For example, perhaps a teenage boy has been told repeatedly (by friends, TV shows, even teachers!) that there is nothing wrong with viewing pornography. Everyone he knows seems to say that doing so is a just normal part of development and that no one gets hurt. If the boy really couldn't be expected to know better and repeatedly views pornography, he may not be personally responsible or guilty for doing so. Still, it is not the case that no harm is done. Pornography seriously harms those who are objectified and commodified, and it harms those who use it. (If the boy views others as objects to be used for selfish reasons, his ability to form meaningful relationships will be compromised.[26])

So even if the boy cannot be held subjectively responsible for his objectively very disordered behaviour, the scenario demonstrates that it is never the case that "ignorance is bliss." In the "real world," evil and injustice have been brought about. Those who have been exploited – and the boy himself – would be much better off if he had understood the true nature and consequences of his actions.

In any discussion about sin, we must remember that "the rules" exist to protect and promote real human goods and values, such as life itself, the dignity of each person, and the full truth of the meaning and purposes of human sexuality. We must know what is truly good to be able to choose it.

It is the Church's mission to proclaim constantly the truth of God's design for human love and life, and to teach what this plan means for each of us. While the Church admits that aspects of this teaching can be very challenging at times, she also proclaims with confidence and joy that God's plan for human life and love – for married love – is ultimately a response to the deepest desires of the human heart: to give and receive unconditional love.

Catholics have a serious responsibility to keep deepening their understanding of what the Church teaches about life in Christ, including marriage and sexuality, to form their consciences in light of this teaching and then to act accordingly. It is true that conscience has "rights," but only because each person's conscience has a serious obligation to seek the full truth of God's loving and liberating plans for us.

Of course, in the end, God alone can judge human hearts. As the Book of Samuel says, "Man looks at appearances, but God looks at the heart." (1 Samuel 16:7) The tradition of Catholic moral teaching also admits that personal circumstances may sometimes reduce (or increase) a person's responsibility for his or her actions: "Imputability and responsibility for an action can be diminished or even nullified by ignorance, inadvertence, duress, fear, habit, inordinate attachments, and other psychological or social factors." (CCC #1735)

Still, we must remember that circumstances in themselves do not change the nature of an act: "they can make neither good nor right an action that is in itself evil." (CCC #1754)

The gift of reconciliation

The sacrament of reconciliation (or penance) is a truly wonderful gift. It does something that years of talk therapy (or alternative medicine or mediated dispute resolution) simple can't do: it restores us to right relationship with God and helps us to grow in true self-knowledge and freedom.

Pope John Paul II underlines the importance of the sacrament, especially for spouses:

> Repentance and mutual pardon within the bosom of the Christian family, so much a part of daily life, receive their specific sacramental expression in Christian Penance. In the Encyclical, *Humanae Vitae*, Paul IV wrote of married couples: "And if sin should still keep its hold over them, let them not be discouraged, but rather have recourse with humble perseverance to the mercy of God, which is abundantly poured forth in the sacrament of Penance." (*Familiaris Consortio* #58, citing *Humanae Vitae* #25)

In other chapters, I have described marriage as a "school of love" and a "school of deeper humanity." Most married people would probably agree that marriage could also be called "a school of forgiving."[27] Those who have experienced Christ's healing forgiveness through the sacrament of Reconciliation will be better able to find forgiveness in their own hearts.

Tragically, however, we all know of situations when it is no longer possible for spouses to live together. For example, in cases of domestic abuse, physical separation may be necessary. But when there is a valid marriage, such separation does not mean that the spouses are no longer married. As members of the same Body of Christ, all members of the Church must offer encouragement and support to those who find themselves in such a painful situation. (CCC #1649, with reference to *Code of Canon Law* 1151–1155)

The question of separation raises the question of the possibility of divorce. In light of what has been said above, it should be clear that if a valid marriage bond has been established, it is impossible to break it. Those who are indeed "married in the Lord" are therefore not free to marry someone else. Even though the marriage bond remains, there are situations where a civil divorce is the only option. For example, a civil divorce is typically required for division of assets, determination of child or spousal support, and other financial responsibilities. (CCC #2383)

For these reasons, the Church cannot recognize as valid the marriage of someone who has divorced and remarried outside the Church, in a civil marriage. There is no denying that such a situation is especially difficult and sensitive. (CCC #1650)

People in this situation may want to explore the possibility of getting an annulment. In some cases, after a church tribunal examines the situation, the Church can declare the "nullity" of a marriage. Annulment (or, more accurately, a "declaration of nullity") is not Catholic divorce. So what is it? It means that, contrary to all appearances, a sacramental marriage never really existed. Something that is essential for a valid marriage was missing at the time the couple exchanged their consent: for example, a lack of capacity because of a personality disorder, a lack of freedom due to coercion, or, from the very beginning, an intention against fidelity or the gift of children). (*Code of Canon Law* 1095–1107) If a declaration of nullity is given, both parties would be free to marry again if their prior obligations are met (CCC #1629, with reference to *Code of Canon Law* 1071)

The gift of the Eucharist

A rich relationship exists between marriage and the Eucharist. Again, we turn to John Paul II for insight:

> The Eucharistic sacrifice ... represents Christ's covenant of love with the Church, sealed with His blood on the Cross. In this sacrifice of the New and Eternal Covenant, Christian spouses encounter the source from which their own marriage covenant flows, is interiorly structured and continuously renewed ... In the Eucharistic gift of charity the Christian family finds the foundation and soul of its "communion" and "mission" .... (*Familiaris Consortio* #57; see also CCC #1655–1658)

Clearly, it would be strange if those who are married "in the Lord" did not seek Jesus and his gift of life-sustaining charity in the Eucharist as often as possible – and preferably as a couple! In the Eucharist, we come to know and love the one whom we are called to imitate.

It may be a cliché to say that the family that prays together stays together. But there is much wisdom in this saying. In fact, the family has its own ecclesial task. It has a unique and essential role to play in the Church and world. The family is sometimes called the "domestic Church" or the "Church in miniature" because, in its own way, it is a "specific realization of ecclesial communion." (*Familiaris Consortio* #21)

In all that they are and all that they do – simply by being an intimate community of life and love – families are a living invitation to encounter Christ.

As the domestic Church, the family must also be a community that worships and a "place" of prayer – a place where all the distractions of modern life are calmed and space is made to focus on the things that matter most and for all eternity. In this, the family may also inspire others (friends, colleagues or even members of the local hockey team) to do the same.

Of course, there is no "perfect" (stress-free, conflict-free) marriage or family life. For us finite and flawed humans, life and love are often messy business! But ironically, it is when couples are struggling the most (perhaps due to unemployment, illness, boredom, or a profound connection with a colleague of the opposite sex) that their example of commitment and steadfastness of heart may be the most compelling. John Paul II adds, "… in a humble and courageous manner, they perform the role committed to them to be a 'sign' – a small and precious sign, sometimes also subjected to temptation … of the unfailing fidelity with which God and Jesus Christ love each and every human being." (*Familiaris Consortio* #20)

Today, more than ever, couples, children and society at large need to see that unconditional love does exist. As Pope John Paul II observes, "To bear witness to the inestimable value and indissolubility and fidelity of marriage is one of the most precious and most urgent tasks of Christian couples in our time." (*Familiaris Consortio* #20) Those who do so are a compelling living response to widespread cynicism or despair about the possibilities for life and love in what is an often fractured world. They show us that there can be tremendous joy in embracing life and love, even when there are real burdens and struggles.

Conclusion

We have covered a lot of ground in a short time. Our point of departure was the view that it is easier to understand the sacramentality of marriage once the basics are in place. So we went on a whirlwind tour of the Church's teaching on creation, sin, our redemption in Christ and the nature of the sacraments – and the Church herself.

As we saw, each of us has been called to a stunningly lofty destiny: to enjoy nothing less than eternal life with the Father, Son and Holy Spirit – and with each other in them. To become the kind of persons worthy of such a destiny, we must grow in our capacity to make a gift of self. In this lifelong journey, Christ is our model – and our way. The good choices we make along the way matter so much because they help us to grow even more in our capacity to love well.

One of the most important choices a person makes is to marry a particular person. Whether you are putting the final touches on the menu and flowers for your big day, or are working through a rocky patch 15 years down the road, I hope that this book has helped you grow in your understanding of what is distinctive about a sacramental marriage. In one word, the difference is Christ! When two Christians marry "in the Lord," their deep human love is infused with Christ's own love. Their marriage becomes a real symbol of Christ's own love. Their love is also transformed, now *actually sharing in* Christ's love for us.

This is good news indeed – and people have a right to hear it! They have a right to hear the beautiful and liberating (if sometimes challenging) truth about marriage "in the Lord." When spouses anchor their life in Christ and draw on the grace of the sacrament, love really is the final word. Even when there is disappointment and heartache (which, inevitably, there will be), there is reason to hope – and "to rejoice always." Christ was at the wedding feast in Cana, and he will be with the spouses at their own wedding celebration – and as they journey through life together.

Why is marriage sometimes described as an "intimate community of life and love"? Because life and love really are inextricably linked. As we have seen (and as experience shows), love is, by its nature, generous and fruitful. So it should not surprise us that the Church teaches that children are the "supreme gift" of marriage. Of course, the love of spouses and families is also fruitful in countless creative ways. Again, that is its nature.

Pope John Paul II called all families – as intimate communities of life and love – to "become what you are." (*Familiaris Consortio* #17) He urged them to commit ever more deeply to their mission of serving love and life. It is my hope that this resource has helped you to think about what might be involved in your own unique mission (and adventure) in service of life and love.

Notes

1. Pope John Paul II's Apostolic Letter *Salvifici Doloris* is a beautiful and thought-provoking reflection "On the Christian Meaning of Human Suffering."
2. Peter J. Elliott, *What God Has Joined ... The Sacramentality of Marriage* (Homebush, NSW: St. Paul Publications, 1990), 32–38.
3. J.A. DiNoia, "*Veritatis Splendor*: Moral Life as Transfigured Life," in *Veritatis Splendor and the Renewal of Moral Theology* (Princeton, NJ: Scepter Publishers, 1999), 1–2.
4. DiNoia, "*Veritatis Splendor*: Moral Life as Transfigured Life," 2.
5. Grisez and Shaw, *Personal Vocation: God Calls Everyone by Name* (Huntington, IN: Our Sunday Visitor, 2003), 98–99.
6. In what has come to be known as his teaching on the "theology of the body," Pope John Paul II has much to say about humanity's "original experience" (before sin) of God's plan for human love.
7. When making reference to this passage, some speak instead of "an intimate community of life and love." This is the case in Pope John Paul II's 1981 Apostolic Exhortation *Familiaris Consortio* ("On the Role of the Christian Family in the Modern World"). In what follows we will do the same.
8. John Grabowski explains further the difference between "covenant" and "contract" in his book *Sex and Virtue: An Introduction to Sexual Ethics* (Washington, DC: The Catholic University of America Press, 2003), 29.
9. For consideration of marriage in the Eastern Rite, see *Code of Canons of the Eastern Churches: New English Translation (Codex Canonum Ecclesiarum Orientalum)* (Washington, DC: Canon Law Society of North America, 2001).
10. To summarize: a valid Catholic marriage requires that 1) the spouses are free to marry; 2) they can and do freely exchange their consent; 3) in giving consent, each spouse intends and promises to create a permanent union, to be faithful to the other, and to be open to the gift of children. This consent is given before an authorized Church minister (priest or deacon) and in the presence of two witnesses. Any exceptions to this last requirement (the "form" of marriage) must be approved by the appropriate Church authority.
11. Elliott, *What God Has Joined*, 146.
12. Elliott, *What God Has Joined*, 167.
13. Elliott, *What God Has Joined*, 167.
14. For example, this is the view of William May, as expressed in his "The Good of the Spouses and Marriage as a Vocation to Holiness" in *The Church, Marriage and the Family* (South Bend, IN: St. Augustine's Press, 2007), 75–94.
15. John Paul II, *Man and Woman He Created Them: A Theology of the Body*, trans. Michael Waldstein (Boston, MA: Pauline Books and Media, 2006).
16. Audience of February 20, 1980.

17 Some of the most popular methods are the Billings Ovulation Method, the Sympto-Thermal Method (STM), which is taught by The Couple to Couple League, and the Creighton Model Fertility Care™ System.

18 Mercedes Wilson compares the effectiveness of NFP with contraceptive methods in her *Love and Family: Raising a Traditional Family in a Secular World* (San Francisco: Ignatius Press, 1996), 246–55.

19 Women who learn how to recognize the true signs of fertility ("fertility awareness") greatly enhance their chances of conceiving. Dr. Thomas Hilgers of Creighton University has developed "NaProTECHNOLOGY" to treat women with sub-fertility, infertility and related medical problems. This approach uses the same "biomarkers" or knowledge of fertility as the Creighton Model FertilityCare™ System, which he and his coworkers also developed. See Thomas Hilgers, *The Creighton Model NaProEducation System*, 3rd ed. (Omaha, NE: Pope Paul VI Institute Press, 1996).

20 See Martin Rhonheimer, *The Ethics of Procreation and the Defense of Human Life* (Washington, DC: The Catholic University of America Press, 2010), 38. Rhonheimer has done much to frame discussion of contraception in light of the virtue of chastity. See also William F. Murphy, Jr., "Forty Years Later: Arguments in Support of *Humanae Vitae* in Light of *Veritatis Splendor*," *Josephinum Journal of Theology*, Vol. 14, No. 2 (Summer/Fall 2007): 122–67 and *Sex and Virtue*, 147–54.

21 See S. Joseph Tham, *The Missing Cornerstone: Reasons Why Couples Use Natural Family Planning in Their Marriages* (Hamden, CT: Circle Press, 2003); Mary Shivanandan, *Crossing the Threshold of Love: A New Vision of Marriage in Light of John Paul II's Anthropology* (Washington, DC: The Catholic University of America Press, 1999); and Janet Smith, *"Humanae Vitae": A Generation Later* (Washington, DC: The Catholic University of America Press, 1991).

22 Discussion of some of the adverse physical (and emotional) side effects for women using chemical contraceptives can be found in Janet Smith and Christopher Kaczor's *Life Issues, Medical Choices* (Cincinnati, OH: Servant Books, 2007). It should also be noted that some forms of contraception can have an "abortifacient" (abortion-causing) effect by preventing the implantation of the embryonic human in the uterus. See John Wilks, "The Impact of the Pill on Implantation Factors – New Research Factors," *Ethics and Medics* 16, No. 1 (2000): 15-22. Smith and Kaczor also discuss this point and suggest many useful resources on contraception and NFP.

23 *Donum Vitae* II (B) 6.

24 Elliott, *What God Has Joined*, 181.

25 Elliott, *What God Has Joined*, 181.

26 Psychiatrist Norman Doidge discusses how viewing pornography actually alters one's brain – and also transforms sexual attractions. See his *The Brain that Changes Itself* (London: Penguin Books, 2007).

27 Elliott, *What God Has Joined*, 185.